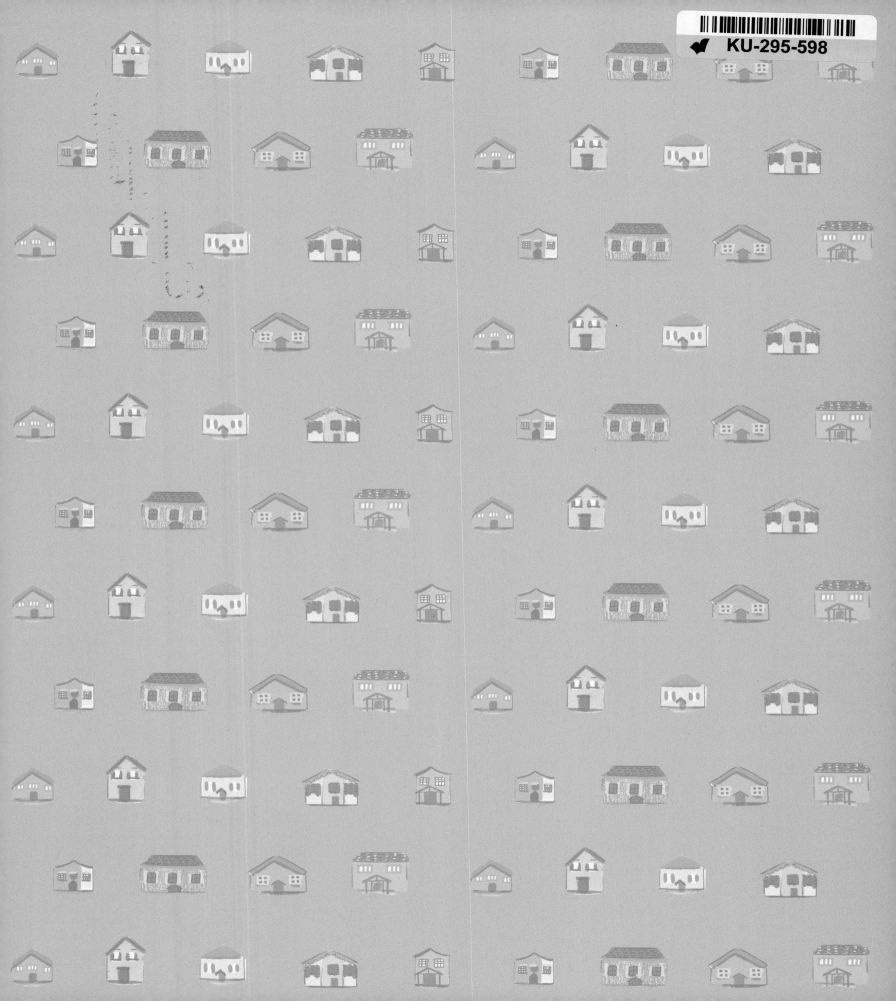

For my mum, who made everywhere home.
M.B.

First published in Great Britain 2019 by Red Shed,
an imprint of Egmont UK Limited
The Yellow Building, 1 Nicholas Road, London W11 4AN
www.egmont.co.uk

Text copyright © Moira Butterfield 2019
Illustrations copyright © Clair Rossiter 2019

The moral rights of the author and illustrator have been asserted.

ISBN 978 1 4052 9186 6

A CIP catalogue record for this title is available from the British Library.

Home Sweet Home

What makes a house a home?

Written by Moira Butterfield

RED SHED

Illustrated by Clair Rossiter

The world is full of different homes,
from tents and huts to bobbing boats
and apartments high up in the sky.

What's your home like?

Is it tall or wide?

How many rooms
does it have inside?

One thing's for sure. It won't
be the same as everybody else's.

So what makes a home a wonderful place?
Is it a roof, doors, walls or cosy beds perhaps?

Let's look around the world and back through
history to find out why homes are so special.

Some homes snuggle together in a street, like a line of friendly faces. Do you know any homes in busy streets and quiet lanes?

The world's busiest cities have the noisiest streets. What sounds would you hear if you lived in a bustling city?

What would you hear if your home was in the countryside?

Streets don't all look the same . . .
The world's most crooked street is
Lombard Street, in San Francisco, USA.
It zigzags eight times so that cars
can get up the steep hill.

One of the longest streets in the world stretches for 500 kilometres through Uruará, Brazil. That's like walking from London to the Scottish border!

Some homes are on water, not on a street. Canal boats moor up next to pathways.

Roofs come in all shapes and sizes.
They may be sloped, flat or even pointy.
What does your roof look like? Do you
know one that looks different to yours?

White storks build big, untidy nests,
sometimes as long as beds, on roofs in
Germany and nearby countries. The
storks are thought to bring good luck.

The town of Sibiu in Romania is famous
for having lots of roofs with eyes! The eyes
are really attic windows shaped like eyelids.

In snowy countries,
houses are often built
with steeply sloping roofs
so that, when it falls,
the snow slips off.

Some people put soil on their roof and
grow plants up there. The soil helps
to keep heat in the house, too, like
a cosy blanket on top of the roof.

In London, UK, there are beehives on the roofs of some apartment blocks. Beekeepers travel round town looking after lots of different beehives and collecting the honey.

Some of the world's oldest homes were built 9,000 years ago in Catalhöyük (cha-tal hay-ook), Turkey. The homes had no doors and there were no streets – people walked around on the flat rooftops.

The Nenets people of Siberia don't have solid roofs on their homes. They live in chums – pyramid-shaped tents covered in reindeer skins.

Many homes have a front door to welcome visitors. What is yours like? Take a look at the homes where you live and pick a favourite front door.

Some farming families in Mongolia, Asia, live in round felt tents called gers. They usually paint their wooden doors lucky orange and decorate them to bring good fortune.

It's considered rude to stand talking in the front doorway of a ger. It's thought to be rather like standing on the neck of the person who lives in the tent.

Not all homes have front doors . . .

Some North African and Middle Eastern Bedouin people live in camel hair tents that they prop open with wooden posts.

A ger is always put up with its door facing south, so that sunlight floods into the tent when the door is opened in the morning.

Walls help to keep out the whirling wind or the blazing sun. They can be decorated, too. If you could decorate a new wall in your home, what would you do?

Lizards occasionally appear on walls inside Indian homes. If the lizard makes a noise - *thik, thik, thik* - while someone is talking, they believe it is a signal that they are telling the truth.

King Louis XI of France thought walls were important when he ruled 600 years ago. He ordered an artist to paint 50 rolls of wallpaper, with angels on a blue background.

When Louis moved home he made sure the wallpaper went with him and was put up wherever he went.

Now you can buy electronic wallpaper that changes from day to day. Electronic circuits are printed on the paper and illuminate tiny lights to make different patterns.

The Achuar people of South America live in the Amazon rainforest between Peru and Ecuador.

They prefer their homes not to have walls, so the buildings stay airy and cool in their hot rainforest location.

Kitchens are often filled with delicious smells and warmth, but they're not all the same. Can you think of a kitchen that looks very different to yours?

Up until 100 years ago in Europe and North America, a dog helped to cook food in the kitchens of grand houses. Meat was roasted on a skewer (a spit) and the dog ran round on a wheel attached to the spit, to keep it turning.

In Vietnam, three gods are said to live in the kitchen. They make a yearly journey to Heaven to report on the people in their home. People try to please them by cleaning the kitchen and putting out little paper hats and boots for them.

Some homes in West African countries don't have kitchens because it's traditional to cook on fires outdoors.

Cooking together outside is a chance for neighbours to get together, chat and share food.

Homes sometimes have a dinner table where people sit to eat food. Where do you like to munch your meals?

Around the world people eat their dinner differently. Some people use knives, forks and spoons. Others use chopsticks and some eat with their fingers.

Chinese emperors once ate with silver chopsticks. They believed, wrongly, that the chopsticks would turn black if the food they touched was poisoned.

In Finland there's a saying: 'Let's put the cat on the table.' It doesn't really mean that a cat gets to sit on the dinner table, though. It's a way of saying: 'Let's tell the truth.'

Long ago, prehistoric people used seashells and pieces of wood to scoop up their food.

If a person spills salt on the table in some European countries, you might see them throw some of the salt grains over their left shoulder. This is to avoid bad luck.

If you ate a traditional celebration meal with a Vietnamese family you might sit on the floor around a bamboo mat instead of a table.

Gardens bring extra visitors – the birds
and bees that like the flowers and trees!
If you could design your own garden,
what would you put in it?

The White House, home of the
US President, opens its gardens to
35,000 visitors for the Easter Egg Roll.
Families take part in an egg-rolling race to
celebrate the Christian festival of Easter.

In Bangladesh, Asia, some families live in low-lying flooded places,
so they grow food for themselves on floating gardens. Their
gardens are rafts made from woven plants and covered in soil.

Paths are very important in Japanese gardens. They are said to make a garden more beautiful and calming.

Many homes around the world don't have gardens, especially if people live in high-rise apartments. Even with no gardens, people like to grow plants in pots on their balconies and windows.

One way of creating a garden inside your home is to hang plants from the ceiling using special upside-down pots. Would you like to try it?

In the Italian city of Milan lots of trees and flowers have been being planted on the balconies of two tower blocks, so they look like a giant garden in the sky. They are called the Vertical Forest.

Stairs can be straight or winding.
Do you know a house with lots of stairs?
Count them next time you climb up.

European rulers once lived in castles with spiral stairs that wound around like a spring.

The stairs were designed to make it hard for enemies to invade. The owners of the castle could run up the stairs, turn round and swing their swords at anyone attacking from below.

People live in apartments high in the sky in the world's tallest building, Burj Khalifa, in Dubai.

They can use the world's longest elevator ride to take them up to their homes, or they could climb 2,909 stairs.
Which one would you choose?

Plenty of homes have no indoor stairs, including treehouses.

Japanese architect Terunobu Fujimori is famous for building treehouses and lives part-time in one, called the Too-High Teahouse.

Bathrooms vary a lot around the world and in history. Do you like having a steamy shower or a bubbly bath in yours?

On the coast of Dubai some homes have an underwater bathroom - you can watch sea creatures swimming by as you wash.

Toilets first became common in European and North American homes around 100-120 years ago. Before that time, people used china bowls called chamber pots. The pots were emptied outside, sometimes into the street!

The wealthiest ancient Romans had bathrooms in their homes but everyone else went to public baths, where they met their friends and chatted while they bathed.

They often spent hours relaxing at the baths, where they could buy snacks and drinks, play board games or exercise.

Do you have a cosy bedroom where you snuggle in your bed? What do you like most about spending time there?

Cesare Mattei moved into Rocchetta Mattei castle in Italy around 160 years ago. He believed pyramids gave energy so he had upside-down mini pyramids built all over his bedroom ceiling.

In China and southeast Asia some people believe that feet shouldn't face the bedroom door. They worry the sleeper's energy might drain out of the room and down the stairs.

The Abenaki people of northeastern North America have a bedtime legend about the beginning of the world.

In northern China people sometimes sleep on a brick platform called a *kang*. Hidden underneath the platform there is a stove that can be lit to heat the kang above.

In their tale, a god slept on a giant turtle and dreamt of all the people and animals in the world. When he woke up he was surprised to find his dreams had become real.

Hammocks are a good way to stay safely asleep in the jungle, away from creepy-crawlies. Sailors once used them for sleeping on their ships.

Astronauts are weightless in space stations, which means they can sleep any way they like. All they need is a sleeping bag attached to a wall so they don't float off.

Have you ever slept in a bunk bed? Bunk beds are sometimes used in bedrooms on board submarines, ships and overnight trains, too, to save space.

In parts of Borneo families share longhouses, with each family having their own space inside. There isn't much room for beds, but people prefer to sleep on mats made from woven bamboo.

So homes are amazingly different around the world, and throughout history as well.

Things like doors and walls, beds and stairs aren't important for everybody, but there *is* something that makes homes special all across the planet . . .

... it's the people we love
and share our homes with!

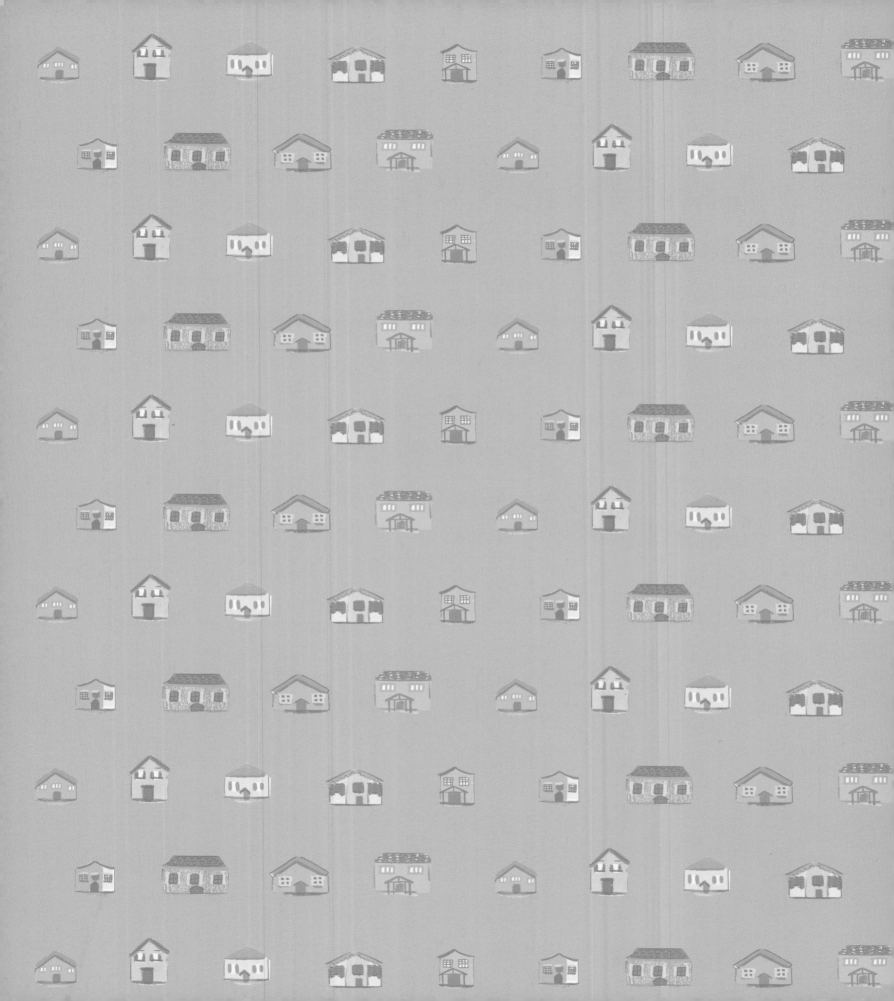

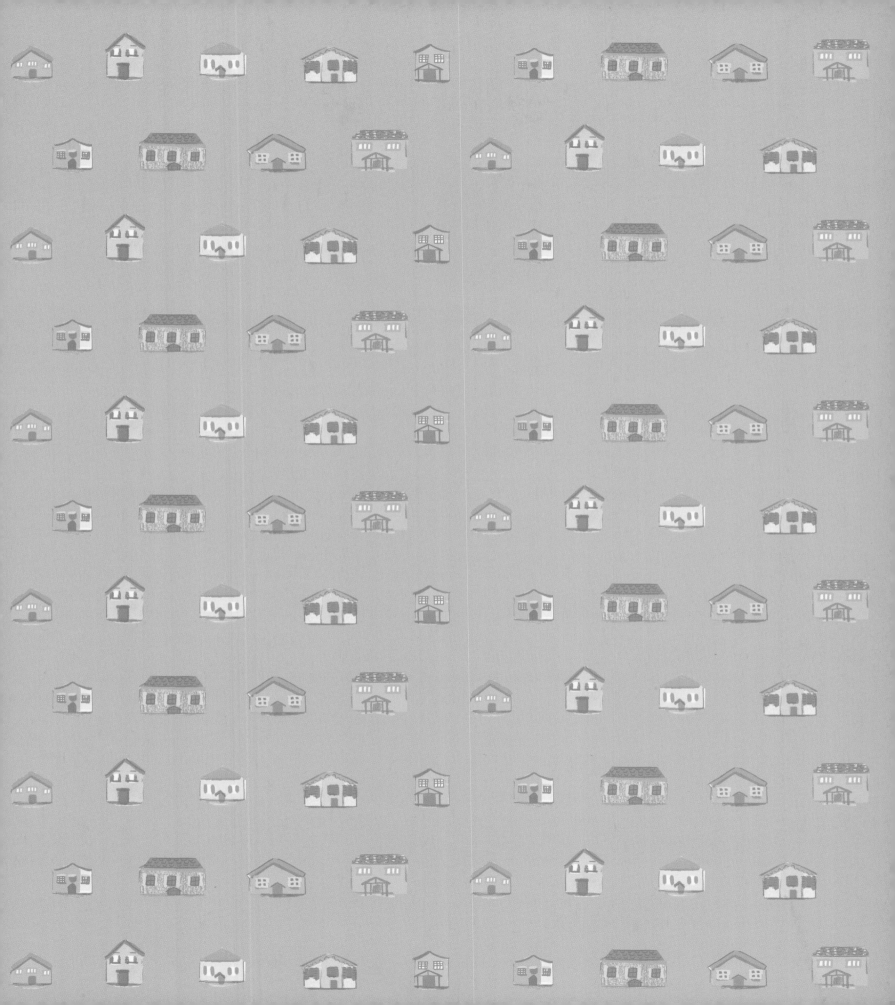